MW00789631

**Discovering
Cultures**

Japan

Robert Reiser

BENCHMARK BOOKS

MARSHALL CAVENDISH
NEW YORK

With thanks to Henry D. Smith II, Professor of Japanese History, Columbia University,
for the careful review of this manuscript.

Benchmark Books
Marshall Cavendish
99 White Plains Road, Tarrytown, New York 10591-9001
Text copyright © 2003 by Marshall Cavendish Corporation
Map and illustrations copyright © 2003 by Marshall Cavendish Corporation
Map and illustrations by Salvatore Murdocca
Book design by Virginia Pope

Library of Congress Cataloging-in-Publication Data

Reiser, Robert.
Japan / by Robert Reiser.
p. cm. — (Discovering cultures)
Includes bibliographical references and index.
Summary: Young explorers will discover the culture of Japan in this lively and easy-to-read text highlighting the country's geography, people, food, schools, recreation, celebrations, and language.
ISBN 0-7614-1177-1
1. Japan—Juvenile literature. I. Title. II. Series.
DS806 .R36 2002
952—dc21   2001007459

Photo Research by Candlepants Incorporated
Cover Photo: Corbis / Michael S. Yamashita

The photographs in this book are used by permission and through the courtesy of; Corbis: Dave Bartruff, 4-5, 13, 17, 21; Steve Kaufman, 6; Michael S. Yamashita, 8, 10, 12, 14, 22, 31, 38-39; Mark L. Stephenson, 9; Charles E. Rotkin, 11; AFP, 15, 34, 41, 44; Walter Hodges, 16; Eye Ubiquitous, 18, back cover; Richard T. Nowitz, 19, 28; Fukuhara, Inc., 20; Ric Ergenbright, 24; Bohemian Nomad Picturemakers, 25; Craig Lovell, 26-27; Reuters NewMedia Inc., 30, 45 (bottom); Robert Holmes, 32-33, 37; Michael Freeman, 36; Bruce Burkhardt, 40; Roger Ressmeyer, 45 (top).

Cover: *A golden temple in Kyoto*; Title page: *A little girl dressed for a festival*

Printed in Hong Kong

1 3 5 6 4 2

Turn the Pages...

Konnichiwa! Irasshai!

(Hello! Welcome!)

Three young competitors gather for a pole-balancing contest.

Where in the World Is Japan?

The islands of Japan curl off the east coast of Asia. A Japanese legend says that a giant catfish sleeps under part of the country, and when he awakens the land trembles and the mountains shake. This story describes Japan. It is a land of earthquakes and volcanoes. One out of every ten volcanoes in the world erupts in Japan. However, most of them, such as the famous Mount Fuji, have been quiet for many years.

Cranes stand in the falling snow in Hokkaido.

Hokkaido

Pacific
Ocean

Honshu

★ Tokyo

Kyoto •
Mount Fuji
• Osaka

Shikoku

Kyushu

N
NW   NE
W   E
SW   SE
S

The four major islands of the Japanese archipelago stretch over a thousand miles from north to south, so the land and weather change from place to place. Hokkaido, the northernmost island, is cold and snowy in the winter, but pleasant and cool in the summer. People from all over Japan travel to Hokkaido to vacation in its pine forests, lakes, and mountains. Honshu, the largest island, has high mountains, deep green valleys, and a temperate climate. The southernmost islands of Kyushu and Shikoku have long hot summers and mild winters, perfect for growing rice.

A boy crosses a lake, as it rains in Kyushu.

Bright signs light up Tokyo at night.

All of Japan's largest cities are on Honshu. Today Tokyo is the nation's capital, and home to ten million people. With its restaurants, theaters, and gleaming lights, Tokyo is as exciting as New York. Kyoto, only two hundred miles away, was

A footbridge stretches across a pond in a Japanese garden.

Japan's capital for more than one thousand years. This historic city is filled with beautiful gardens and ancient temples. Osaka, a large seaport and industrial center, has been an important commercial city for four hundred years.

Mount Fuji

One of the world's most famous volcanoes, Mount Fuji, is only a short train ride from Tokyo. This 12,380-foot (3,773-meter) mountain has been quiet for almost three hundred years. The Japanese consider Mount Fuji to be a sacred peak and a symbol of rebirth. Millions of people visit the mountain to climb or admire its beauty. For the last one thousand years, poets, artists, and now photographers have tried to capture Mount Fuji on paper. For that reason, almost everyone has seen a picture of this national treasure.

What Makes
Japan Japanese?

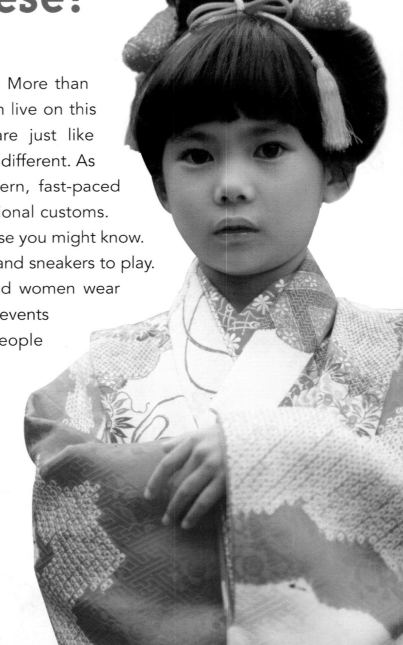

The people make Japan Japanese! More than 126 million men, women, and children live on this island nation. In many ways they are just like Americans. In other ways they are very different. As much as Japanese people love modern, fast-paced living, they also appreciate their traditional customs.

People usually dress like anyone else you might know. Children wear pants or shorts, T-shirts, and sneakers to play. For work, men wear business suits and women wear dresses and skirts. However, for special events such as weddings and festivals, people sometimes wear traditional dress.

For important occasions, women might wear *kimono*. These silk robes are held together with special sashes called *obi*. For formal occasions, men

*Girls often attend festivals
wearing colorful kimono.*

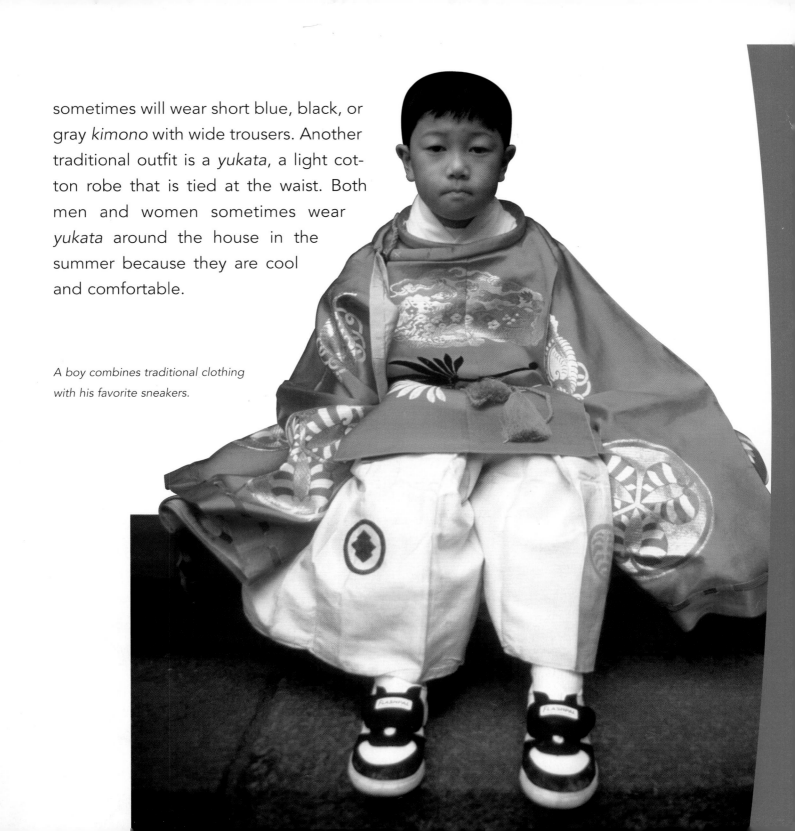

sometimes will wear short blue, black, or gray *kimono* with wide trousers. Another traditional outfit is a *yukata*, a light cotton robe that is tied at the waist. Both men and women sometimes wear *yukata* around the house in the summer because they are cool and comfortable.

A boy combines traditional clothing with his favorite sneakers.

What else makes Japan Japanese? Teamwork! Since ancient times, the Japanese people have depended on rice for food. Farmers had to make sure that they had a good crop every year, or many would go hungry. Farmers grew rice in paddies, land that is covered by water. Because they shared common ponds to water their rice paddies, the farmers depended on one another. They worked together to build and maintain the paddies. From this grew the Japanese tradition of teamwork, which has helped make this small island nation into one of the most important countries in the world.

Workers plant rice in a paddy in Kyushu.

Japan has given many gifts to the United States. Popular foods such as *sushi* and *tempura* and sports such as *karate* and *judo* come from Japan. The beautiful cherry blossoms that decorate Washington, D.C., were also a gift from Japan.

Japan is well known for its automobiles and electronics. Some of the most popular cars in the world come from Japanese automakers such as Toyota and Nissan. Televisions, compact disc players, and video games come from Japanese companies such as Sony. Even the world-famous Pokémon and Pac-Man are Japanese computer game characters!

Children show off their video games.

A grandmother and granddaughter make origami *cranes.*

Artists are an important part of Japanese culture. People make kites, paint, or do calligraphy for the joy of making something beautiful. *Origami* is one of the most popular arts in Japan. People of all ages love to fold paper into beautiful shapes like animals, birds, and flowers. One favorite *origami* shape is the crane. It is supposed to bring long life and good fortune. An old legend says that a sick person can be healed with one thousand paper cranes.

Chopsticks

In the past, people often prepared Japanese food to be eaten without cutting, so they used chopsticks when they ate. Today, the Japanese also use forks, knives, and spoons. As soon as modern Japanese children can hold chopsticks in their hands, they learn to eat with them. Here's how:

1. Hold the upper chopstick like a pencil, about one third of the way from the top.
2. Line up the second chopstick, pointing the same way, resting on the ring finger and on the base of the thumb.
3. Move the upper chopstick with the thumb and the index finger to pick up food. The bottom chopstick never moves.

17

Living in Japan

A traditional Japanese home is usually smaller than an American home, but the rooms feel open and comfortable. Many homes have beautiful gardens or collections of potted plants. Most people like to feel close to nature, even in the city, so they spend many hours carefully tending their plants.

The outside of a traditional Japanese house.

Children are surrounded by shoji *as they play cards in their* tatami *room.*

Traditionally, Japanese people sat on the floors of their homes. Today some Japanese homes have carpeted floors, but many people prefer to leave their wooden floors uncovered. Most houses or apartments will have a *tatami* room. *Tatami* are large woven mats that are placed on the floor. The rough inside of a *tatami* is made from rice straw. The outside is covered by a finely-woven reed that is smooth and comfortable to sit on. When the outer covering of a *tatami* gets dirty, it can be turned inside out.

A Japanese home is not crowded with big heavy furniture. Instead of sitting on large armchairs, people may sit on cushions called *zabutons*. Instead of a bed, most people sleep on mattresses called *futons*, which can be folded and put away during the day.

For privacy, rooms are divided by *shoji*, screens that slide out from the wall. They are made of light wood and paper or cloth, so it is important not to make a lot of noise in the house. With so little space, it is also important to keep the home tidy. When people come in from the outside, they take off their street shoes and put on slippers, called *surippa*.

Mealtime is important in Japan. Rice is a big part of every meal. In fact, the Japanese word for rice, *gohan*, has also become the word for a meal. *Asa-gohan* (morning rice or breakfast) might be a bowl of rice and a special soup with tofu and seaweed called *misoshiru*. *Hiru-gohan* (lunch) might be sandwiches, a salad, or flavored rice balls.

For *ban-gohan* (supper) the family gathers around a dining table. If they have a *tatami* room, they sit on cushions and begin their meal by saying, "*Itadakimasu*." (Thank you for the food.) An evening meal

Chopsticks rest on top of a plate holding a gourmet Japanese meal.

A Japanese family sits on zabutons *around the dinner table.*

might be grilled or fried fish, with cooked vegetables, a salad, and of course, rice. But families don't always eat just Japanese food. They also enjoy foods like spaghetti and hamburgers. On special occasions, they might share *sukiyaki*, a delicious hot casserole of rice noodles, vegetables, and meat. After dinner, people say, "*Gochiso sama deshita.*" (Thank you for the delicious meal.)

A father cuts cake for his daughter.

Let's Eat!
Chicken Yakitori

This Japanese recipe is delicious and very easy to make. Ask an adult to help you.

For sauce:

1/4 teaspoon ginger powder
(or 1/2 teaspoon chopped fresh ginger root)

1/4 teaspoon garlic powder

1/4 teaspoon onion powder

1 tablespoon brown sugar

2 tablespoons soy sauce

1/4 cup mirin
(Japanese sweet cooking wine)

One chicken breast

Wash your hands. Mix together the ingredients for the sauce. Set aside. Cook the chicken breast. (Be sure it is fully cooked and not pink.) Allow the chicken to cool and then cut into one-inch chunks. Place the chicken in a small casserole dish and cover with sauce. Put it in the refrigerator for at least one hour. Next, slide the chunks of sauce-covered chicken onto wooden skewers or bamboo sticks. (You can buy them at a cooking store or a Japanese grocery store.) Set them on a hot grill. Brush with the leftover sauce. Turn over after three or four minutes and grill the other side. Serves four.

23

School Days

Education is a very important part of Japanese life. Children go to *shogakko* (elementary school) Monday through Friday, and on Saturday morning. Because most people live close to schools, children usually walk. Crossing guards help them across busy streets. To be extra safe, children wear bright yellow caps as part of their school uniform so that drivers can see them easily.

These yellow hats warn drivers to steer clear of students.

Once in school the *sensei* (teacher) calls the class to order. *"Ohayo gozaimasu"* (Good morning), he or she says, and all the children stand up and bow. In Japan good manners are very important, and bowing is a sign of respect when greeting a parent, teacher, or an elder.

The *sensei* teaches math, social studies, and language. In addition to studying Japanese, children learn the same alphabet that is used in English. Japanese is not an easy language. Every student must learn to read and write forty letters, as well as hundreds of *kanji*. *Kanji* are characters taken from ancient Chinese writing. Each *kanji* represents one whole word. Using a special pen, children write *kanji* with carefully placed strokes. This art is called calligraphy.

Lunch period is just as special in Japan as it is in any school in the world. At lunchtime, two to four children leave

A student wears her uniform to school.

Children draw during an outdoor art class.

the classroom to get the lunches, while everyone else puts away their books. The assigned students walk to the lunchroom and place the meals for their class on carts. Then they bring the lunch carts to the classroom. The students and the *sensei* sit down together and eat sandwiches or noodles and vegetables, followed by a sweet cake for dessert. Afterward, everyone cleans up and gets ready for recess in the school yard.

In Japanese schools, children also participate in sports, music, and art. Students might play baseball or soccer. In music class they learn to play harmonicas. Many children also take private music lessons at home to study the violin, piano, or *shamisen* (Japanese banjo). In the art room, the *sensei* teaches painting, kite making, or puppet making.

Japanese parents are very involved in their children's education. They meet with the *sensei* several times a year to

Parents help their son with his homework.

find out what their children are studying and what they can do to help. And once or twice a year the *sensei* visits the students' homes to get to know their families better. This kind of cooperation between teachers and parents encourages Japanese children to do their best.

Haiku

The Japanese write a special kind of poetry called *haiku*. These three-line poems come from a party game that Japanese people played over three hundred years ago. First, everyone sat in a circle and one person started a poem. The next person tried to make a link, or connection, to what the person before him had said. The game continued around the circle. Sometimes the poems were funny. Sometimes they were very beautiful. Today both children and adults love to write *haiku*.

The secret of writing *haiku* is to remember that it is as much a picture as a poem. It shows us a scene and lets us fill in our feelings. The first line usually describes a tiny picture, the second line tells us more, and the third line gives a little surprise:

Golden sunbeams
Touch the sparkling water
Remember to laugh.

Can you write one? Remember—three lines of five, seven, and five syllables, and one single idea with a surprise at the end.

Just for Fun

An Olympic judo competition

Japanese children work hard, but when school is out they love to play games, such as *nawatobi* (jump rope), *kakurenbo* (hide-and-seek), and *ayatori* (cat's cradle). They also enjoy *menko*, a game played with *samurai* or monster picture cards.

Some children spend time at a special school called a *dojo* to learn traditional Japanese martial arts, such as *judo* or *karate*. One of the most popular martial arts is *kendo*, a sport that grew from the sword fighting of *samurai* warriors hundreds of years ago. Today, children and adults both learn *kendo*. They

Kendo *students practice their moves during a martial arts class.*

dress in dark blue gear with padding. Like figure skaters, *kendo* competitors leap and dance as they strike with their long wooden swords.

Sumo wrestling is a very old sport in Japan. Wrestlers are powerful men weighing more than three hundred pounds who have trained since they were very young. At the start of each match, salt is thrown over the ring. Then the wrestlers take their positions and begin. When the match ends, each wrestler bows to his opponent.

Not all of Japan's sports are old. *Besuboru* (baseball) is the most popular team sport in the country. Just as in the United States, major league teams compete for a World Series championship. Over 15 million people go to stadiums each year to watch the games.

Japanese children love comic books. Every month, dozens of comics called *manga* magazines appear on the stands. There are special *manga* for everyone. Boys read *shonen manga* and girls read *shojo manga*. Teenagers and adults read romance *manga* and science fiction *manga*. The color and style of these Japanese cartoons are internationally known. Some

A junior league baseball team celebrates a winning season.

Customers read the comics at an Internet cafe.

manga artists have created characters such as Astro Boy, whose adventures are followed by children around the world.

Recently, Japanese children have begun greeting one another with the words *"Oh-ha!"* The regular way of saying good morning is *"Ohayo gozaimasu,"* sometimes shortened to *"Ohayo"* among friends. *"Oh-ha!"* is the greeting of Shingo Mama, a favorite TV character played by Shingo Katori, a six-foot-tall man wearing a wig and a frilly apron. Every week, Shingo Mama dresses up and makes a surprise visit to one of her fans. She makes breakfast, clowns with the children, and sends them off to school. Her greeting is always a cheerful, *"Oh-ha!"*

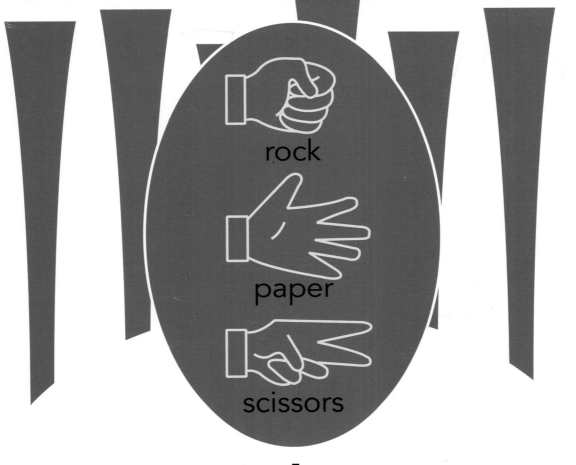

rock

paper

scissors

Janken

Janken is the Japanese version of Rock-Paper-Scissors. It is a quick way to decide who will go first in a game. Players hide one hand behind their backs and make the shape of rock (fist), paper (flat hand), or scissors (two fingers). Then they shout *"Janken pon!"* and show their hidden hands. Rock always breaks scissors, scissors cuts paper, and paper covers rock. You have probably tried the game of Rock-Paper-Scissors. Next time try it the Japanese way and shout *"Janken pon!"*

Let's Celebrate!

The Japanese celebrate many festivals and some of them are especially for kids! November 15 is a holiday for children who are seven, five, and three years old. It is called Shichi Go San (Seven-five-three). On this day, three- and five-year-old boys and three- and seven-year-old girls dress up in colorful *kimono*. Some boys wear tuxedos. They are given paper bags filled with candy. The children visit Shinto shrines with their families to pray for their good health.

Traditionally, there were separate holidays for Japanese boys and girls. Many families still celebrate them today. The girls' holiday is called Hina Matsuri (The Doll Festival) and the boys' holiday is Tango no Sekku, now known as Children's Day.

Many Japanese girls look forward to Hina Matsuri on March 3. They dress up in traditional *kimono* and display dolls dressed in ancient

Girls dress in traditional kimono *for Children's Day.*

Japanese dolls and miniature furniture on display in a museum

Japanese court costumes. They surround the dolls with miniature household furnishings. *Hina* doll collections are passed on from mothers to daughters. They are sometimes very old and precious. When a baby girl is born, one of the best gifts she can receive is a *Hina* doll.

On May 5, Children's Day begins with a visit to a Shinto shrine or a Buddhist temple. Shinto and Buddhism are Japan's most important religions. After asking for blessings for their family, children promise to work hard for the next year. Cloth streamers shaped like carp fish are flown like flags from tall buildings. Boys and their families also tie the carp streamers outside their homes. The streamers seem to swim against the wind, just as the carp swims against the current in rivers. The carp is famous in Japan and China for its strength, dedication, and long life.

An ancient Buddhist celebration, O-Bon comes in July or August. It lasts for about a week, but the actual dates vary between regions. O-Bon is a time when people gather with their families to pay respect to relatives who have died. The air is filled with music, and lanterns float down the rivers and decorate the outside

Carp windsocks are flown in celebration of Children's Day.

of houses. The lanterns are lit to greet the spirits of departed ancestors at the beginning of the festival and to send them on their way at the end. An important O-Bon event is the Bon Odori, when people dressed in *yukata* gather in town parks or shrines to dance in a large circle.

The biggest of all Japanese festivals is O-Shogatsu (New Year's). This holiday lasts for five days, including New Year's Eve and New Year's Day. Schools and most businesses are closed for the first three days of the new year so that people can return to their hometowns to celebrate with family and friends. The Japanese visit shrines and eat special meals prepared ahead of time, so that no one has to cook during the holiday. Families and friends wish each other *"Akemashite omedeto gozaimasu!"* (Happy New Year!)

Japanese lanterns hang from homes during O-Bon.

Kite Festivals

On New Year's Day and again during the Hamamatsu and Showamachi festivals in May, the sky above Japan is full of red, yellow, and black kites soaring and dipping like beautiful birds. The Japanese word for kite is *tako*, so people who love to fly kites are called *tako-kichi*, which means kite-crazy.

Over two million people each year watch the Hamamatsu festival. Teams from different towns bring specially decorated giant kites. Then, men dressed in costumes make their fighting kites fly at one another. The strings on their kites are covered with sharp bits of glass, so they can cut the strings of the other kites in the air.

For the Showamachi festival people build the world's largest kite. It is 40 feet (12 meters) wide and weighs over two thousand pounds. It takes two hundred youngsters to raise this kite into the sky. When the great cloth-and-wood bird finally catches the wind, the temple bells ring and thousands of spectators cheer!

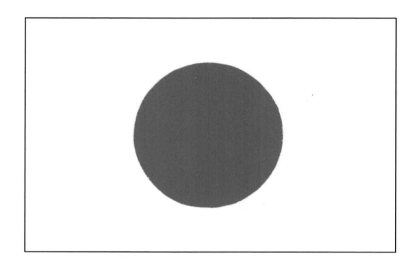

The colors of the Japanese flag are red and white. The red circle represents the sun in the center of a white field.

In the United States, money is measured in dollars and cents. In Japan, they use Yen. There are Yen coins and banknotes (paper money). Some Yen coins have holes in them. That's because, long ago, the Japanese strung their coins together and carried them around their necks.

Count in Japanese

English	Japanese	Say it like this:
one	ichi	ee-chee
two	ni	nee
three	san	sahn
four	shi	shee
five	go	goh
six	roku	roh-koo
seven	shichi	shee-chee
eight	hachi	hah-chee
nine	ku	koo
ten	juu	joo-oo

Glossary

archipelago   Group of islands.

calligraphy (kuh-lih-gruh-fee)   Artistic writing with a brush and ink.

irasshai (ee-ra-shy)   Welcome greeting.

judo (joo-doh)   Martial art for self-defense without weapons.

karate (kah-rah-tee)   Unarmed fighting using the hands and feet as weapons.

kendo (ken-doh)   Fencing with bamboo swords.

kimono (kee-moh-noh)   Traditional Japanese robe with wide sleeves.

konnichiwa (kohn-nee-chee-wah)   Hello in Japanese.

manga (mahn-gah)   Comic books.

obi (oh-bee)   Broad sash worn with kimono.

* Individual syllables are not stressed when pronouncing Japanese words.

Proud to Be Japanese

Kouji Hanada, also called Takanohana (1972–   )

One of the most widely recognized men in Japan today weighs 350 pounds (159 kilograms). He is Takanohana, the country's most popular *sumo* wrestler. Born in Tokyo in 1972, he was given the name Kouji Hanada. His grandfather, one of the best-known Japanese wrestlers of modern times, competed under the name of Takanohana. In 1988, young Kouji first wrestled professionally. The crowd was so impressed that they asked him to take his grandfather's wrestling name. With his brother who fights under the name Wakanohana, Kouji has helped keep this traditional sport popular.

Akira Kurosawa (1910–1998)

Japan's most famous film director began his career as a struggling painter. Akira Kurosawa was born in 1910 in a comfortable home in Tokyo. He loved art, so

44

instead of studying to become a schoolteacher like his father, he spent all of his time painting. Even when he failed the exam to go to Japan's leading art school, he continued to paint. Finally, he found fulfillment as a film director. His most famous films, such as *Rashomon* and *Seven Samurai*, are set far back in Japan's history. They tell stories of courageous men who fought great odds to achieve their dreams. Akira Kurosawa's work inspired filmmakers in Europe and America, and made Japan one of the movie capitals of the world.

Seiji Ozawa (1935–   )

Another famous Japanese person made his name with a conductor's baton. Seiji Ozawa was born to Japanese parents living in China, but he was educated in Japan. At the Tokyo Toho School of Music, Ozawa learned the skills that would make him one of the best-known orchestra conductors in the world. Since then, he has made hundreds of recordings as the conductor of the Boston Symphony, the Tanglewood Festival, the New York Philharmonic, and dozens of the world's best orchestras. He is considered one of the greatest musicians in the world today.

Find Out More

Books

AA to Zen: A Book of Japanese Culture by Ruth Wells. Simon & Schuster, New York, 1992.

Japanese Children's Day and the Obon Festival by Dianne M. MacMillan. Enslow Publishers, New Jersey, 1997.

Postcards from Japan by Zoe Dawson. Raintree Steck-Vaughn Publishers, New York, 1996.

This Place Is Crowded by Vicki Cobb. Walker & Company, New York, 1993.

Web Sites

http://jin.jcic.or.jp/kidsweb

Kids Web Japan features Japanese stories, games, recipes, and pen pals, and a "What's Cool" section about all the latest Japanese fads and fashions.

http://www.tecnet.or.jp/~haiku

The *Children's Haiku Garden* has poems from children all over the world. They encourage young poets to send them their latest works to publish on the Web.

Video

My Neighbor Totoro, 20th Century Fox, VHS, 1996.

Index

Page numbers for illustrations are in **boldface.**

About the Author

Bob Reiser, award-winning author and professional storyteller, has been telling tales and writing them down since his boyhood in Brooklyn, N.Y. His books with Pete Seeger, *Carry It On* and *Everybody Says Freedom*, are read across the country. His children's book, *David's Got His Drum*, co-written with Panama Francis, was published by Marshall Cavendish in 2002. He lives in Tarrytown, N.Y. with his wife Sandy, his son William, and his daughter Robin.